3 1833 05330 3787

P9-EEN-342

Stories
of
GREAT PEOPLE

Shakespeare's quill

Gerry Bailey and Karen Foster

Illustrated by Leighton Noyes
and Karen Radford

🍄 Crabtree Publishing Company
www.crabtreebooks.com

Mr. RUMMAGE has a stall piled high with interesting objects—and he has a great story to tell about each and every one of his treasures.

DIGBY PLATT is an antique collector. Every Saturday he picks up a bargain at Mr. Rummage's antique stall and loves listening to the story behind his new 'find'.

HANNAH PLATT is Digby's argumentative, older sister—and she doesn't believe a word that Mr. Rummage says!

Mr. CLUMPMUGGER has an amazing collection of ancient maps, dusty books, and old newspapers in his rare prints stall.

Crabtree Publishing Company
www.crabtreebooks.com

Other books in the series

Cleopatra's coin

Columbus's chart

Martin Luther King, Jr.'s microphone

Leonardo's palette

Armstrong's moon rock

The Wright Brothers' glider

Marco Polo's silk purse

Mother Teresa's alms bowl

Sitting Bull's tomahawk

Credits

British Library, London/Bridgeman Art Library: 17 bottom
Corpus Christi College, Cambridge/Bridgeman Art Library: 33 top
Mary Evans Picture Library: 10 top, 12 top, 15 top right, 17 top, 18 top, 18 bottom, 27 top, 28 bottom, 35 top
Mark Furness Collection/Mary Evans Picture Library: 31 bottom
NPG, London/Topfoto: 20 top
Picturepoint/Topham: 20 center left, 31 top
Private Collection/Bridgeman Art Library: 19 top, 33 bottom
Private Collection/Christies Images/Bridgeman Art Library: 15 bottom left
Private Collection, ©Rafael Valls Gallery, London/Bridgeman Art Library: 23 top
Arthur Rackham/Mary Evans Picture Library: 12 bottom
R. Sheridan/Ancient Art & Architecture Collection: cover, 19 bottom, 26 bottom
Topfoto: 23 bottom, 27 bottom
Victoria & Albert Museum, London/Bridgeman Art Library: 9 top

Picture research: Diana Morris info@picture-research.co.uk

Library and Archives Canada Cataloguing in Publication

Bailey, Gerry
    Shakespeare's quill / Gerry Bailey and Karen Foster ; illustrated by Leighton Noyes and Karen Radford.

(Stories of great people)
Includes index.
ISBN 978-0-7787-3691-2 (bound).--ISBN 978-0-7787-3713-1 (pbk.)

    1. Shakespeare, William, 1564-1616--Juvenile fiction. 2. Dramatists,
English--Early modern, 1500-1700--Biography--Juvenile fiction.
I. Foster, Karen, 1959- II. Noyes, Leighton III. Radford, Karen
IV. Title. V. Series.

PZ7.B15Sh 2008   j823'.92   C2007-907627-0

Library of Congress Cataloging-in-Publication Data

Bailey, Gerry.
    Shakespeare's quill / Gerry Bailey and Karen Foster ; illustrated by Leighton Noyes and Karen Radford.
        p. cm. -- (Stories of great people)
    Includes index.
    ISBN-13: 978-0-7787-3691-2 (lib. bdg.)
    ISBN-10: 0-7787-3691-1 (lib. bdg.)
    ISBN-13: 978-0-7787-3713-1 (pbk.)
    ISBN-10: 0-7787-3713 6 (pbk.)
    1. Shakespeare, William, 1564-1616--Juvenile literature. 2. Dramatists, English--Early modern, 1500-1700--Biography--Juvenile literature. I. Foster, Karen, 1959- II. Noyes, Leighton, ill. III. Radford, Karen, ill. IV. Title. V. Series.

    PR2895.B35 2008
    822.3'3--dc22
    [B]
                                          2007051261

Crabtree Publishing Company
www.crabtreebooks.com   1-800-387-7650

Published in Canada
Crabtree Publishing
616 Welland Ave.
St. Catharines, Ontario
L2M 5V6

Published in the United States
Crabtree Publishing
PMB16A
350 Fifth Ave., Suite 3308
New York, NY 10118

Published by CRABTREE PUBLISHING COMPANY
Copyright © 2008 Diverta Ltd.

All rights reserved. No part of this publication may be reproduced, stored in a retrieval system or be transmitted in any form or by any means, electronic, mechanical, photocopying, recording, or otherwise, without the prior written permission of Crabtree Publishing Company.

Shakespeare's Quill

Table of Contents

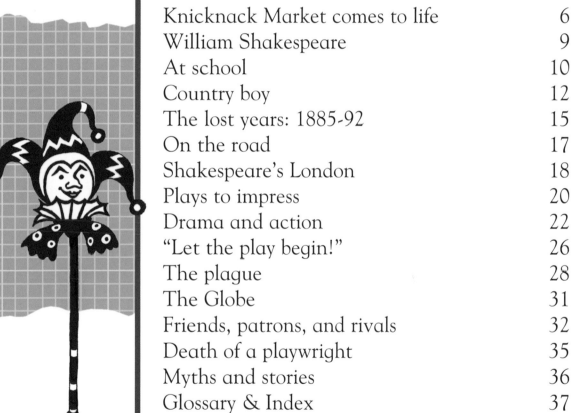

Every Saturday morning, Knicknack Market comes to life. The street vendors are there almost before the sun is up. And by the time you and I are out of bed, the stalls are built, the boxes are opened, and all the goods are carefully laid out on display.

Objects are piled high. Some are laid out on velvet: precious necklaces and jeweled swords. Others stand upright at the back: large, framed pictures of very

important people, lamps made from tasseled satin, and old-fashioned cash registers—the kind that jingle when the drawers are opened. And then there are things that stay in their boxes all day, waiting for the right customer to come along: war medals laid out in straight lines, stopwatches on leather straps, and utensils in polished silver for all those special occasions.

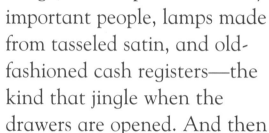

But Mr. Rummage's stall is different. Mr. Rummage of Knicknack Market has a stall piled high with a disorderly jumble of things that no one could ever want. Who'd want to buy a stuffed mouse? Or a broken umbrella? Or a pair of false teeth?

Well, Mr. Rummage has them all. And, as you can imagine, they don't cost a lot!

Digby Platt—ten-year-old collector of antiques—was off to see his friend Mr. Rummage of Knicknack Market. It was Saturday and, as usual, Digby's weekly allowance was burning a hole in his pocket.

But Digby wasn't going to spend it on any old thing. It had to be something rare and interesting for his collection, something from Mr. Rummage's incredible stall. Hannah, his older sister, had come along too. She had secret doubts about the value of Mr. Rummage's objects and felt, for some big-sisterly reason, that she had to stop her little brother from buying useless bits of junk.

But as Digby and Hannah walked down the street, they saw their friend standing outside the rare prints stall, talking to the owner, Mr. Clumpmugger.

"Hi Mr. Rummage. Hi Mr. Clumpmugger," they said together.

"Well, look who's here—my two favorite customers!" said Mr. Rummage in a cheerful voice.

"Hello there," said Mr. Clumpmugger with a smile. "A nice day for bargain hunting, don't you think?"

"It sure is, but I'm not really looking for a print today," said Digby. His eye had been caught by what looked like a large feather sticking out of a pot. "But I might be interested in this feather..." Digby picked it up and examined it.

"Oh no!" said Hannah. "Digby, put it down. It's a ratty old feather, that's all. Don't waste your money on silly things like that."

"Actually, it's a goose-feather **quill**," said Mr. Rummage, "and it's not exactly silly. Mr. Clumpmugger will back me up on this. That quill you're holding belonged to none other than the brilliant English playwright, William Shakespeare!"

William Shakespeare

William Shakespeare was born in 1564. He grew up in the busy market town of Stratford-upon-Avon in England, where he lived in a comfortable home on Henley Street. The family name of Shakespeare is very old and was probably pronounced "Shaxpere" by William.

William's parents

William's father, John Shakespeare, worked as a glove maker and as a timber and wool merchant. He was also the Mayor of Stratford. John married Mary Arden, the daughter of a local landowner. Together they produced seven children. William was the third.

He grew up to become a respected actor and writer in his own lifetime. William Shakespeare is now regarded as the greatest English **playwright** of all time.

Let's find out more...

At school

Shakespeare went to King's New Grammar School in Stratford-upon-Avon, where he was given a classical education. It was tough at school in those days. He studied Latin and Greek and spent hours learning long passages from ancient books by heart. Lessons in logic and debating helped him think clearly and argue well, while public speaking lessons taught him to speak clearly and go on to write stirring speeches for the characters in his plays. Eventually, Shakespeare used his lively imagination to plan clever plays and write wonderful poetry. But, like most young men, he often got bored in school and longed to escape from his strict teachers so he could play games outside with his classmates.

Stratford-upon-Avon

William Shakespeare's signature

Money troubles

When Shakespeare was 12, his father's business failed, and John Shakespeare was put in prison for owing someone money. Young William would have been upset by his father's money problems. In fact, as he grew up, he worked hard so that, one day, he'd be able to restore his family fortunes. By the time he left school, Shakespeare was determined to make a successful business out of writing plays.

Religious upbringing

Each Sunday, young William went to church with his parents. He heard the priest chant prayers, he listened to the psalms sung by the choir, and enjoyed reading aloud from the Bible. His religious upbringing may have helped develop his love for spoken language.

"William Shakespeare!" exclaimed Hannah. "I really like his plays, especially *A Midsummer Night's Dream.* We went to see it in the park last year."

"I had to stay at school," grumbled Digby. "I bet Shakespeare never had to sit in a rotten old classroom."

"Ah, but he did," said Mr. Rummage. "And his lessons were probably far more difficult than yours, my boy."

"That's right," agreed Mr. Clumpmugger. "It was a long, hard day. Lessons started at dawn, and went on well into the evening."

"Sounds terrible," shuddered Digby. "What did they study all that time?"

"Some of the things you do, like math and English," said Mr. Rummage. "But they also studied ancient Greek and Latin, old languages we don't speak today. Luckily, Shakespeare was very clever and he had a huge vocabulary—around 30,000 words."

"Well, that's about 29,990 more than Digby," giggled Hannah. "Oh really?" said Mr.Clumpmugger disapprovingly. "Anyway, when you think that the average kid today uses around 3,000 words, you can see the difference." "I hate spelling tests," said Digby.

"You're not the only one, Digby," said Mr. Clumpmugger. "But remember, once you've learned how to spell a word, you'll never forget it. Then you'll be able to read and enjoy stories by great writers like Shakespeare—and that'll be fun."

Country boy

We know that Shakespeare loved the countryside because in many of his plays he refers to the changing seasons and accurately describes wild flowers, birds, and animals. His colorful poetry brought his plays to life.

Spirits of springtime

The Forest of Arden near Shakespeare's home may have inspired him to write *A Midsummer Night's Dream*. This popular play is set in an enchanted forest where woodland spirits and fairies come out to play and make flowery speeches to each other. The play was put on during May Day celebrations, when rural areas celebrated nature and the coming of spring with feasts, dancing, and entertainment.

Posies and poisons

In Shakespeare's dark and tragic play, *Hamlet*, the crazed Ophelia, makes fantastic bouqets of "crow flowers, nettles, daisies and long purples". And in *Cymbeline*, the wicked queen sends her ladies into the fields to collect primroses, violets, and cowslips to make a deadly poison.

Fields and woods

Shakespeare also used his love of nature to bring his characters and scenery to life. In his famous play about two unlucky lovers, *Romeo and Juliet*, he describes Juliet as "the sweetest flower in all the field". And in his ghost story "Macbeth," he describes evening as a time when "light thickens, and the crow makes wing to the rooky wood."

The young poacher

When Shakespeare wasn't sitting at his writing desk, he liked to go out hunting and fishing with his friends. According to legend, he was once caught killing a deer in Charlecote Park, the home of a nobleman called Thomas Lucy. In those days, all deer belonged to the king or queen of England, so anyone caught killing or eating one would be punished. But young Shakespeare wasn't sorry and apparently called Lucy an "ass" and a "scarecrow," and made up a rhyme about him:

"If lousy as Lucy, as some folk miscall it
Then Lucy is lousy, whatever befall it."

The story goes that Lucy threatened to put Shakespeare in prison which is why he fled to London. But it's probably not true.

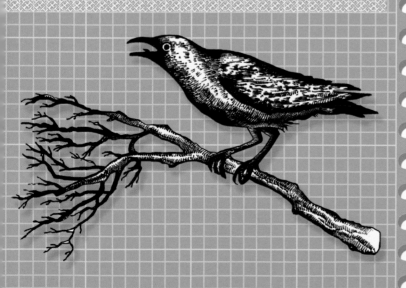

"What did Shakespeare do when he wasn't at school?" asked Digby.

"Well," began Mr. Rummage, "he would have gone for long country walks and picnicked in the fields and forests near his home. In those days, country people made their own entertainment. Young William would have enjoyed archery, hunting, village games, and going to country fairs."

"Sounds good to me," said Hannah.

"And when he had nothing better to do," added Mr. Clumpmugger, "he probably sat under a shady tree and composed poems and love letters to his girlfriend."

"Did Shakespeare start writing plays when he left school?" asked Digby.

"No, that came later," said Mr. Rummage. "But we do know that he got married rather quickly. He was only 18 but his bride, Anne Hathaway, was already 26—which was old to be getting married in those days. Anyway, a few months after their wedding, Anne gave birth to their first child, Susanna. We don't know much about Anne. But she was probably the eldest daughter of the Hathaways of Shottery, a tiny village not far from Shakespeare's home. Today there's a thatched farmhouse in the village called 'Anne Hathaway's Cottage.'"

"So did he settle down, to be a dad?" asked Digby.

"No one knows. That's why the first years of his married life are often called the "Lost Years." There've been plenty of books written about what he might have done—but it's all guesswork."

"What did people think he did, then?" asked Hannah.

"All kinds of things, apparently," laughed Mr. Clumpmugger. "He could've been a butcher's boy, a lawyer, a traveling actor, a soldier, a sailor... You name it, he's supposed to have done it!"

The lost years: 1885-92

Early marriage

William and Anne had two more children, Judith and Hamnet. In fact, the hero of Shakespeare's tragic play *Hamlet* was named after Hamnet, who died at age 11. We know very little about Shakespeare's wife. She may have brought a dowry of money, or been a "good catch," but we'll never know. What we do know, however, is that Shakespeare chose to spend most of his married life in London, faraway from his family.

Dead-end jobs?

Many people have tried to guess what Shakespeare did during the Lost Years. Some say he was a lawyer because his plays show knowledge of the law. Others think he was a gardener because his characters know so much about nature. But that would have been true of most rural people. He probably wasn't a doctor either, because he didn't like them—in one play he wrote "Throw the physic to the dogs!" It's much more likely that Shakespeare helped his father by trading wool or barley in the marketplace. Or that he may have lent a hand in the family's glove-making business. After all, he did have a wife and family to support.

Lure of the stage

At some point, Shakespeare fell in love with the theater. Perhaps he'd seen the traveling theater visiting Stratford before pleading to go on stage himself. At some point he decided to go to London to seek his fame and fortune.

"Shakespeare must have been pretty brave to just leave his family and head off for London," said Hannah. "He was very young, wasn't he?"

"Yes, but he must've known what he really wanted to do and that he'd have to go to London to do it. In fact, once he got there, he joined up with a company of actors called the Queen's Men. It was exhausting work as a new play had to be performed every day."

"I could do that," said Hannah enthusiastically as she struck a pose. "I could be a fairy princess or a warrior queen. But you...," she added, pointing to Digby, "would be the **court** jester."

"I don't want to be the jester," cried Digby, who was trying on some finger puppets. "I'd be king of the castle, and you'd be my chambermaid, or a groom in my stables."

"That's a job for smelly little boys like you," snarled Hannah. "Off with his head!"

Dangerous business

You might think that sitting down and writing a play was a fairly safe thing to do. But in **Elizabethan** times, it wasn't. Plays were often written for famous people, or even the king or queen. They contained scenes on political events and religion that might please some people but make others very angry. If a powerful person was upset they could have a playwright thrown into jail, or even executed as a **traitor**.

A playwrights craft

When he joined the Queen's Men troupe in London, Shakespeare probably spent most of his time writing out speeches, learning his lines, and rehearsing for performances. He may have begun by rewriting old plays—adding scenes or bringing them up to date. Then he would have started to write his own, choosing the actors, and the parts they were to play.

On the road

At first, Shakespeare may have joined a troupe of actors, or "players", and toured the country-side. On feast days in Elizabethan times, people looked forward to the arrival of the traveling theater. Actors, musicians, jesters, and acrobats would often perform on large horse-drawn stages called pageant-cars. Shakespeare would have lived fairly rough and performed in all kinds of weather. And if the spectators didn't like the show, they'd have made rude jokes or pelted him with rotten vegetables!

Traveling theater companies set up stage on the village green.

In Shakespeare's day, theaters were noisy, exciting places where spectators joined in with the performance.

Inns and taverns

Once the curtains closed at the end of a performance, young Shakespeare and his actor friends relaxed in the **taverns** south of the River Thames. It is said they would talk "with subtle flame and wit"—although they probably weren't as refined and sober as some paintings suggest! The players and producers drank ale, laughed rowdily, told dirty jokes, and chased barmaids. Actors, on the whole, didn't have a good reputation—and probably with good reason.

Shakespeare's London

In Elizabethan times, London was the only real city in England, with a quarter of a million inhabitants. That would be just a small city today. But London was very crowded and people lived in cramped houses built close to each other and overlooking narrow, dirty streets. City life was unhealthy and probably frightening for a countryman like Shakespeare. But its busy streets were alive with people going about their business. Young William probably started out by renting a cheap room in a tavern.

Shakespeare was fascinated by the big city. Every day, he would visit the playhouses on both sides of the river Thames.

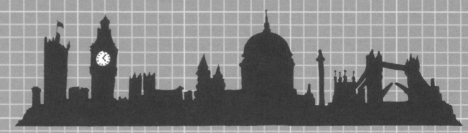

Landmarks

Many of London's landmarks appeared in Shakespeare's plays, especially The Tower of London— England's most feared jail. In its dank cells and torture chambers, prisoners awaited their death. Outside, the heads of traitors were stuck on spikes for everyone to see. Shakespeare included plenty of action, high **treason**, and blood and guts in his plays to appeal to his Elizabethan audiences.

3 1833 05330 3787

Street life

The sights and sounds of London would have excited Shakespeare—street vendors peddling their pies and puddings, town criers ringing their bells and tradesmen singing out their wares. Sometimes royal pageants passed through the streets—uniformed soldiers, members of the court on horseback, and perhaps even Queen Elizabeth in her golden carriage, dressed in robes of silk and fur with jewels to match.

Londoners would line the streets when Queen Elizabeth went out with attendants from her courts.

City entertainment

Most Elizabethan pastimes were bloodthirsty and cruel. Bear-baiting, cockfighting and hunting hares took place in the gardens around Southwark. Shakespeare probably preferred to visit the playhouses on the riverbank. Early theaters, like the Swan and the Rose, were based on the circular bear gardens and cockpits nearby. Most were built by merchants, which probably inspired Shakespeare to build a theater of his own later on.

Shakespeare based some of his characters on the Londoners he saw around him.

19

Plays to impress

Sometimes plays were written to impress or flatter the **monarch**. When Shakespeare wrote his history plays, he made sure that he didn't insult the royal family. So he would change the time, place, and even the events to make the Tudors, Elizabeth I's family, look good. Then, when James I came to the throne, he did the same for the Stewart family.

James I

Elizabeth I

Costumes

In Elizabethan times, it was against the law to wear clothes above your social rank. Only actors were allowed to break the law and dress up like royalty. A lot of money was spent on spectacular costumes, and the "tireman," or person responsible for the wardrobe was important. Wardrobes included fine clothing and jewelery. Colors were important, as they showed rank. Scarlet, for example, was worn by nobles and members of the church, while blue was worn by merchants and servants.

Masques and music

Court performances usually included a masque. A masque was a rich and spectacular entertainment that included music and poetry and was performed in fantastic costumes. Huge amounts of money were spent on masques, and often the audience joined in—even the king or queen. It was an excuse to dress up and wear masks. Performers recited poetry, sang, and danced in front of an elaborate set.

"Did the king or queen ever visit the playhouses where Shakespeare was working?" asked Hannah.

"No," answered Mr. Rummage, "they were too high and mighty for that. But they liked their entertainment as much as ordinary people. So they ordered the actors to come to court."

"Wow, I'd have liked to have done that," said Digby. "Did they get to sit on the throne and wear a crown and stuff?"

"If they wanted to get beheaded, they did," sniffed Hannah, with her nose in the air.

"Right," said Mr. Clumpmugger. "They performed in the banqueting halls of the palace or out in the royal gardens. Plays and parties were organized by the Master of Revels and put on at Christmas or Easter— or whenever the court was bored."

"And they played for the **patrons** who sponsored them too," added Mr. Rummage. "Players had to have a patron, or they might be arrested as street people and whipped or jailed."

"Is that why Shakespeare went to work for the Lord Chamberlain's Men—so he had support?" suggested Hannah.

"You're right. Although there were a lot of other acting companies, including Lord Strange's Men, Lord Pembroke's Men, The King's Men, and The Lord Admiral's Men," said Mr. Rummage.

"It was acting at court that probably taught Shakespeare a lot about court life," said Mr. Clumpmugger. "He soon learned what information he could write into his plays and what he should leave out. He didn't want to step on anyone's toes—and you couldn't be too careful with all the gossiping and secret plotting that went on behind everyone's back."

"**P**lays can be difficult to understand, though," said Digby. "I prefer action movies and thrillers."

"You should see him when he's watching a horror movie," teased Hannah. "He hides behind the couch when things get scary."

"No I don't!" grumbled Digby.

"Well, Shakespeare wouldn't have disappointed either of you then," said Mr. Rummage. "He loved horror stories too. In his first play, *Titus Andronicus*, which is set in ancient Rome, Titus's daughter Lavinia, walks onstage with her hands cut off and her tongue cut out. Later on Titus kills the men who did it, cooks them, and serves them up in a pie to their mother!"

"Gross!" shivered Hannah. "That's horrible."

"Can we go and see *Titus Andronicus*?" asked Digby.

"You can go, if you want to," said Hannah, "but I want to see the history plays."

Drama and action

During Shakespeare's lifetime, England was often at war and people were used to violence and bloodshed. Public executions were common, noble families plotted to take over the throne, others planned to blow up the Houses of Parliament, and the royal court was full of dangerous gossip. Shakespeare used the events around him to add drama to his plays and excite his audiences. Although he had read history books, he was far more interested in action and drama than in being accurate.

Actors had to be in great shape if they wanted to star in Shakespeare's history plays, which contained deadly duels, swordfighting, and full-blown battles.

Staged battles

In 1588, the Spanish king sent a huge fleet of ships to invade England. It became known as the Spanish Armada. Shakespeare would have been 24 years old when the battle was fought and he probably helped celebrate the English victory. He later wrote 10 history plays based on English kings and the battles they fought to win the throne. The plays were all box office hits—they kept the monarch happy, and William's audiences thoroughly enjoyed cheering on the heroes and booing the villains.

The good, the bad, and the ugly

Shakespeare's royal characters aren't all brave and honorable heroes. Some, like Richard III and Macbeth, are greedy, murderous villains. Others, like Hamlet, are sad and mysterious. And some, like King Lear, are just plain foolish.

Elizabethan audiences wanted to see battles on stage, especially when England was at war. They enjoyed having something to cheer about.

"It must have been tough for the players to learn all those lines," said Hannah.

"I bet you'd forget yours," laughed Digby.

"Very funny," said Hannah. "I'd have a lot of fun being a heroine, though."

"The theater WAS a lot of fun," interrupted Mr. Rummage, "but it was hard work too. The players were expected to act more than one character in each play. And William's plays were packed with characters—heroes and villains, knights and members of the court, kings and queens, masters and servants."

"And they all had funny names, too," added Mr. Clumpmugger. "There's Bottom and Pistol, then there's Mistress Overdone, Mopsa, Froth, Shallow, Simple, and many, many others."

"You'd be Simple," Hannah said, looking down her nose at Digby, "or Bottom."

"Can we dress up as the characters?" Digby asked Mr. Rummage, ignoring his sister.

"Of course,"said Mr. Rummage. "Come on, let's see what I've got in my costume box..."

Hannah and Digby followed Mr. Rummage to his stall and watched as the antiques dealer opened a pair of large wooden trunks full of theater costumes.

"Here's one for you, Hannah" said Mr. Rummage, pulling out a flowery dress.

"This is the fairy queen's costume from *A Midsummer Night's Dream*. And guess what? Here's the donkey's costume from the same play. Go on, Digby, play the part."

"What do I have to do?" asked Digby, slipping on the donkey's head.

"Act silly," giggled Hannah. "That should be easy enough for you!"

"That was great," said Mr. Rummage. "Now, how about dressing up as the wicked witches in *Macbeth*?"

"Oh yes, can I try on the green nose? Hey, that hat really suits you, Digby!" giggled Hannah.

"And so does your straggly green hair!" hooted Digby.

"Hubble, bubble, toil, and trouble..." they chanted.

"Woooo! over here, Hannah! I'm William Shakespeare, the headless ghost!"

"Digby!" squealed Hannah. "You scared me by hiding in the neck **ruff** of that suit!"

"Can we do another comedy now?" asked Digby. "This is really heavy stuff..."

Mr. Rummage laughed. "Well, you could always try one of these pointed hats with bells and be a clown or a jester. Even in Shakespeare's more serious plays there were clowns called fools who made the audience laugh. But they weren't so foolish. They were often the wisest and most important characters in a play."

"Let the play begin!"

Elizabethan theater

Like all of us, Elizabethans wanted to have fun. Their lives were often difficult and death, diease, or misfortune were never faraway. As well as entertaining themselves, Elizabethans looked forward to shows put on by traveling performers. In these shows, musicians, clowns, and acrobats, as well as actors, performed plays.

Many of these were morality plays, which taught moral lessons about everyday life. The actors played with words, giving them different meanings to make people laugh. Wit and poetry were popular, but there was also room for the rough and tumble of slapstick comedy, which added some relief to a sad story.

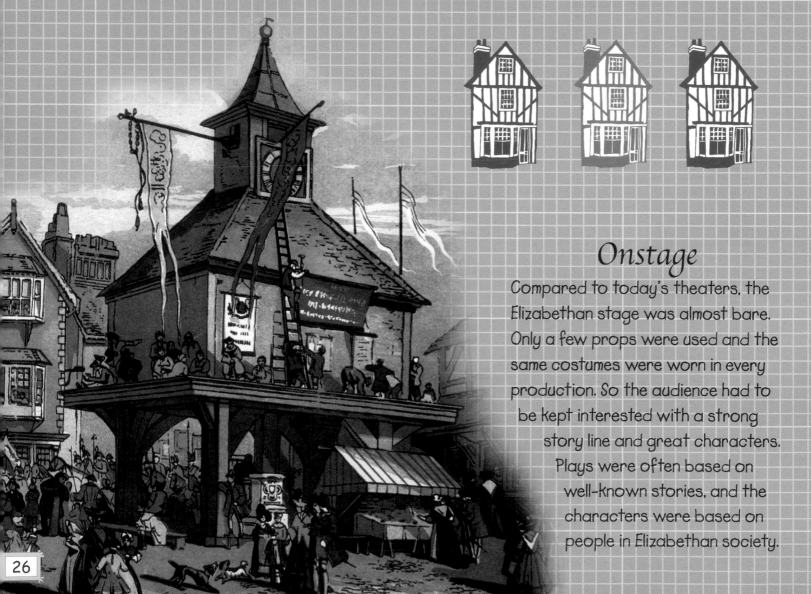

Onstage

Compared to today's theaters, the Elizabethan stage was almost bare. Only a few props were used and the same costumes were worn in every production. So the audience had to be kept interested with a strong story line and great characters. Plays were often based on well-known stories, and the characters were based on people in Elizabethan society.

The audience

The stage of an Elizabethan theater was usually set up in the yard outside a tavern. The yard offered standing room only, and it cost a penny to get in. This is where the poorer tavern workers, apprentices, and shopkeepers stood. They were often rowdy, and threw rotten fruit at the stage whenever an unpopular character came on. Wealthy theater-goers, such as merchants, paid more to sit in the gallery. Comfortable seating was provided for ladies and gentlemen who paid even more. There were also lord's rooms, for the **nobility**.

Fairy tales and ghost stories

Shakespeare used myths, fairy tales and ghost stories to make his plays special. In *A Midsummer Night's Dream*, we meet a whole society of imps and fairies. In *Macbeth*, we meet three witches who warn Macbeth of his deadful fate. And in *Hamlet*, the hero is haunted by ghosts from his past. In those days, ordinary people loved to see magic and horror being acted out on stage.

Tragedies

Shakespeare based his tragedies on Greek and Roman stories. Tragedies don't have a happy ending. Usually they are about revenge or family fights. But Shakespeare made his tragedies great by adding a human touch. We can understand his characters and what they are going through and we feel upset by their tragic end.

Comedies

Comedies are plays with a happy ending. There's often a moral lesson to be learned too. Most of Shakespeare's comedies involve playing tricks on the hero and heroine, who have to work through all sorts of problems and misunderstandings until they finally forgive each other and marry. The stories end with the feeling that *All's Well that End's Well*.

The plague

A terrible **plague** hit England in 1348 and wiped out a third of the population. Even in Shakespeare's day, England was never safe from disease—especially London. Public playhouses were shut down from time to time and plays were banned by law if more than thirty people died in one week.

Secret drama

Even though times were tough, Londoners still looked for some kind of entertainment. So when playhouses were closed, the theater took to the streets. Shows had to be performed secretly. Troupes even left the city and toured the countryside to get away from the plague—although, unfortunately, they often carried it with them to the villages they played in.

Shakespeare the poet

When the playhouses closed for two years, William turned to writing poetry rather than plays. Poets were even more respected than playwrights, especially if they had a noble patron. William's patron was the Earl of Southampton.

The sonnets

Shakespeare wrote a series of famous poems called sonnets. Together, they tell the story of a poet's struggle to find real meaning in his life and how difficult this turns out to be.

"Most people died of fever within a few days of the plague starting."

"And of course no one knew what caused it," added Mr. Rummage. "There was no known cure and just the slightest contact with a sick person might make you fall ill."

"So that's why the theaters had to close." said Mr. Clumpmugger. "It was dangerous to have so many people close together in one place. If just one of them was carrying the disease, hundreds might catch it. London was particularly at risk because there were so many people living in a small area."

"**W**ere the playhouses open every day?" asked Digby.

"Most days," said Mr. Rummage, "but often they were shut down for long periods."

"Why was that?" asked Digby.

"Well, sometimes playhouses were closed because religious people didn't approve of them—and sometimes because of the plague..."

"I've heard about the plague," interrupted Digby excitedly. "People got bitten by huge rats. Then their skin fell off..."

"They turned purple first, though," added Hannah.

"Not quite," said Mr. Clumpmugger, "although what really happened was just as bad—large boils and black and blue blotches appeared all over the body.

Rummage's
"Antiques"

"Did Shakespeare work in a big theater?" asked Hannah.

"He did," said Mr. Rummage. "Most of his plays were staged at a playhouse called The Theatre, on the north side of the river Thames—but unfortunately, he didn't get along with the manager, James Burbage."

"So what happened? Did Shakespeare get fired?" asked Digby.

"Not exactly, but he got annoyed because Burbage was always hiring and then firing him whenever he felt like it. Anyway, when Burbage died, his playhouse was closed down and, all of a sudden, Shakespeare was left with nowhere to perform.

According to legend, Shakespeare and his friends dismantled The Theater in the dead of night. Then they used a rowing boat to move the timber across the river to Southwark, on the south side of the Thames, where they rebuilt it. The playhouse was renamed The Globe, and it became famous for staging Shakespeare's plays."

"He and his friends became owners of half of The Globe," continued Mr. Clumpmugger. "The other half was owned by Burbage's brothers, who were in on the plan to move the theater in the first place! But Shakespeare soon realized that running a theater was an expensive business."

The Globe

The Globe playhouse was a circular building made of timber and plaster. It had no roof and so it was open to the weather. The stage opened out into a space called the yard. Behind the stage was the "tiring house" where the actors dressed in their costumes. Above this was an upper acting area called the "heavens" and on top of that, a platform for performers. Around the yard were three tiers of galleries and also special rooms for gentlemen. Actors entered or left the stage from the tiring house. There was also a trapdoor on the stage floor, known as the entrance to "Hell."

Scenery, props, and costumes

Elizabethan theaters didn't use complicated scenery. But they did have moveable props such as tombs, beds, and a great horse with legs. Actors could also be raised or lowered from the stage by a kind of winch. Costumes, on the other hand, were plush and showy. Special effects included fake body parts, such as hands and heads, bladders full of "blood", smoke, and canon fire. Fire was dangerous, though, and in the end, it was a fire that caused The Globe playhouse to burn down.

Romeo declares his love for Juliet in a famous balcony scene.

The actors

Actors had to learn their lines quickly. They also had to be able to learn many different plays at once, as one performance often followed straight after another. Actors often had more than one role to play and, because women weren't allowed on stage, female roles were acted by young boys.

Friends, patrons, and rivals

At the tavern

The Mermaid Tavern, located off Friday Street in the London part of Cheapside, was rented by a literary group that called itself the Friday Street Club. On the first Friday of each month it became the meeting place for actors, authors, playwrights, and poets including Christopher Marlowe, Ben Jonson, John Donne, Sir Walter Raleigh, and, of course, William Shakespeare.

Shakespeare enjoyed meeting fellow writers and poets at London's popular Mermaid Tavern.

Christopher Marlowe

Christopher Marlowe was born in the same year as William Shakespeare and, like him, became a great Elizabethan playwright. But unlike Shakespeare, Christopher was reckless. As well as writing plays, Marlowe also worked as a spy for Queen Elizabeth's secret service. His murder in a tavern brawl when he was just 28 may have been carried out because of his work as a spy. Shakespeare, on the other hand, managed to stay out of trouble.

A good manager

Unlike many of his fellow actors, Shakespeare became prosperous as well as famous. He was well paid for his plays and with the money he earned he invested wisely in property—as well as in The Globe playhouse. He bought the second biggest house in his hometown of Stratford and was made a gentleman with his own coat of arms. At last he was able to go back to his family and write from home.

"It must have been fun being an actor in Shakespeare's day," said Digby. "You could do all kinds of things like act, write plays, sing, or fire a canon."

"If you did that you'd probably kill half the performers and most of the audience," laughed Hannah.

"Yes, that could be dangerous," agreed Mr. Rummage. "But there were other risks too. Many people were jealous of Shakespeare's popularity—and they envied the fact that he wrote his plays so quickly and easily. And then there were the religious Puritans, who didn't like people having fun."

"Did they stop Shakespeare from writing?" asked Digby.

"No, but they tried to," said Mr. Rummage. "Puritans thought the theater was evil because it made people act out of character. It's what a play is all about really!"

"Crazy," sighed Hannah.

"Yes, but unfortunately, many Puritans held high positions in public life. For instance, the Puritan Lord Mayor of London said that playhouses were meeting places for thieves, horse stealers and plotters of treason." It was easy for him to shut down a playhouse and put the actors out of work. And that could mean starvation, or even jail. Which is why theater companies needed the backing of a powerful noble, or even the king himself. That's why Shakespeare's company was renamed the King's Men—so they had the backing of James I and could be safe."

"As long as they didn't upset the king, of course," added Hannah.

"Precisely. For example, when a play called *The Isle of Dogs* was put on, it angered the royal family because it was full of insults. As a result, the playhouses were closed and the actors, including the notorious Christopher Marlowe, were jailed."

"I bet Shakespeare really enjoyed writing plays for his new theater," said Digby.

"Yes, many of his most famous plays were written especially for The Globe," said Mr. Rummage.

"Do you think he used this quill to write all of his plays?" asked Digby.

"Not all of them," replied Mr. Rummage. "Quills didn't last that long. But he probably used it to write his last play, *The Tempest*."

"Hmm," said Hannah. "I wonder if any of Shakespeare's magic rubbed off on that quill?"

"I wouldn't be surprised," said Mr. Clumpmugger. "After all, *The Tempest* is a magical play. Everything takes place in just one afternoon."

"Then I will buy the magic quill, and this afternoon I will write a play even better than *The Tempest*," said Digby in his best Shakespeare voice.

"Listen to him," laughed Hannah. "It'd take him all afternoon just to write his address!"

"That's not true!," replied Digby. "Here's a dollar for your quill, Mr. Rummage. With it I will create something that is truly wonderful."

"More likely something weird, if you ask me," laughed Hannah. "Come on, clown, it's time to go home. Goodbye Mr. Rummage, goodbye Mr. Clumpmugger," shouted Hannah as she pulled her brother and his precious quill away.

Death of a playwright

The Globe Theater burned down in 1613, but it was rebuilt a year later. Shakespeare didn't live long enough to spend a lot of time in it, though. He died in 1616, on April 23, the same day of the month he was born.

William's will

On March 25, 1616, Shakespeare signed his will. He wasn't well and he died a month later. He had made a small fortune from writing plays and he was generous to his friends and relatives. His daughter Susanna got most of his estate. Oddly enough, he only left his wife "my second best bed with the furniture," which seems odd. However, in those days, wives were usually looked after automatically, and the best bed would have been reserved for guests anyway.

Epitaph

Shakespeare must have been worried that, at some time in the future, someone might want to dig up his grave. So he asked for a message to be written on his tombstone:

"Good friend for Jesus sake forbear To dig the dust enclosed here Blest be ye man who spares these stones And curst be he who moves my bones."

35

Myths and stories

Many myths and stories have grown up around Shakespeare since his death. Find out what is fiction and what is fact below.

Fiction: William Shakespeare was poorly educated and couldn't have written plays with so many classical references.

Fact: Shakespeare was very well-educated. Jealous writers probably started this story.

Fiction: In his youth, Shakespeare was a butcher's apprentice.

Fact: This is unlikely as he was too well-educated to do such a job.

Fiction: In order to write his first work, Shakespeare traveled around Italy with a troupe of Italian actors.

Fact: He may have gone to Italy, but there is no proof of this.

Fiction: Shakespeare was a secret Catholic.

Fact: This is unlikely as he was baptized, married, and buried with Church of England ceremonies. None of his children was thought to be Catholic. The supposed testament of his father, John, was a fake.

Fiction: When he first went to London, Shakespeare worked with horses.

Fact: This myth was meant to make Shakespeare seem unsophisticated. Again, jealous writers probably started this story.

Fiction: Shakespeare was married to another Anne.

Fact: The Bishop of Worcester's clerk entered the wrong name of the bride in the register before the day of the marriage. He wrote Anne Whatley of Temple Grafton, instead of Anne Hathaway.

Glossary

court The place where a king or queen lives; a royal mansion or palace

Elizabethan The time during which Elizabeth I of England was queen; describing events or styles that occurred while Elizabeth I was queen

monarch One who rules over a state or territory, usually for life, who is in power because he or she was born into a royal family

nobility A class of persons distinguished by high birth or rank

patron A person who supports, protects, or gives money to someone or something

performer An entertainer who traveled from place to place, especially to sing and recite poetry.

plague A highly infectious disease that causes death

playwright A person who writes plays

quill A feather that is sharpened and dipped into ink to make a writing pen

ruff A stiffly starched frilled or pleated circular collar, worn by men and women in the 16th and 17th centuries

tavern An inn for travelers and also a place where alcoholic drinks can be sold and drank

traitor A person who betrays his or her country, a cause, or someone's trust, especially one who helps one's enemies

treason A group of touring actors, singers, and/or dancers

Index

Other characters in the Stories of Great People series.

KENZO the barber has a wig or hairpiece for every occasion, and is always happy to put his scissors to use!

BUZZ is a street vendor with all the gossip. He sells treats from a tray that's strapped around his neck.

COLONEL KARBUNCLE sells military uniforms, medals, flags, swords, helmets, cannon balls—all from the trunk of his old jeep.

SAFFRON sells pots and pans, herbs, spices, oils, soaps, and dyes from her spice kitchen stall.

Mrs. BILGE pushes her dustcart around the market, picking up litter. Trouble is, she's always throwing away the objects on Mr. Rummage's stall.

CHRISSY's vintage clothing stall has all the costumes Digby and Hannah need to act out the characters in Mr. Rummage's stories.

PRU is a dreamer and Hannah's best friend. She likes to visit the market with Digby and Hannah, especially when makeup and dressing up is involved.

YOUSSEF has traveled to many places around the world. He carries a bag full of souvenirs from his exciting journeys.

JAKE is Digby's friend. He's got a lively imagination and is always up to mischief.

PIXIE the market's fortuneteller sells incense, lotions and potions, candles, mandalas, and crystals inside her exotic stall.

Mr. POLLOCK's toy stall is filled with string puppets, rocking horses, model planes, wooden animals— and he makes them all himself!